Encouragement Along The Way

A Devotional Guide & Journal

for Home-Schooling Parents

Bobbie Howard

Foreword by Cathy Duffy

Noble Publishing Associates

Noble Publishing Associates, the publishing arm of Christian Life Workshops, is an association of Christian authors dedicated to serving God and assisting one another in the production, promotion, and distribution of audio, video, and print publications. For instructions on how you may participate in our association, or for information about our complete line of materials, write to:

Noble Publishing Associates
P.O. Box 2250
Gresham, Oregon 97030

or call (503) 667-3942.

ISBN: 1-56857-028-7
Printed in the United States of America.

FOREWORD

"Praise be to the God and Father of our Lord Jesus Christ, the Father of compassion and the God of all comfort, who comforts us in all our troubles, so that we can comfort those in any trouble with the comfort we ourselves have received from God. (2 Cor. 1:3-4)

Encouragement is the currency of true friendship. It is the act of kindling hope in a heart that has grown cold from adversity. Encouragement provides a moment of calm and clear thinking in the midst of all the craziness. Anyone who is engaged in an important quest needs encouragement on a regular basis. Home schooling parents are no exception.

Unfortunately, for many a home school mom, the emotional bank account can get pretty low sometimes. It is so easy to become weary with well doing and forget why we decided to teach our children at home in the first place. That is what Bobbie Howard experienced as a young wife and home schooling mother in the pressures and multiple moves of military life. With little in the way of on-going, face-to-face friendships, she found it necessary to turn again and again to "the God of all comfort." The result is not only comfort and encouragement for her own heart, but for ours as well.

As I have watched the growth and development of the home-school movement, I have noticed how quickly we get caught up in questions about teaching methods and curricula. My own books have certainly contributed to that process. But as important as those issues are, when you are in the trenches across from a fierce line of home-school students having a bad day, the choice of your curricula might have nothing to do with your success or failure that day. At that point what really makes the difference is the relationship you have in your heart with Jesus Christ. It all comes down to why are you doing this?

If it's just for the sake of the kids, well, they won't much appreciate it today, thank you very much. If it's to strike a blow against the enemy (e.g. public schools, ACLU, etc.), they don't seem to be paying much attention. If it's for our own ego gratification, we'll find a very hollow reward. Ultimately, we have to know in our heart of hearts that what we are doing is for the Lord, and that He is the One Who wants us to do this. Then, even though it won't be easy, we can rest assured it will be good, and that we will reap if we don't give up, not because we are such great teachers, but because He is Lord of the Harvest. This is the encouragement Mrs. Howard shares with us.

In the process of turning our eyes to Jesus, we also get a nice helping of Bobbie Howard and all her ideas, insights and observations about what home school moms go through at home, at church, in the neighborhood and even with the school authorities. The next time the lady at the grocery store, or the in-laws, or the "sister" at church asks us a probing question about home schooling, we'll be able to share from the added insight we've gained from Bobbie; it's like consulting with a friend before facing life's challenges.

Bobbie, herself, is quick to say that hers is not the high-sounding prose of some great devotional writer from ages past. She's a mom just like us. These are her day to day ponderings and observations, shared with dashes of wit and wisdom, from the kitchen table of a real home school family. Day by day, as Bobbie shares her thoughts and insights about this adventure we call home schooling, something wonderful begins to happen. We become friends. When she gets indignant about something, so do we. When she laughs, we laugh. And when she reaches out for help to the One Who makes it all make sense, we get a better grip on God, too.

The new format of her book encourages us to join in this process by writing our own thoughts and feelings about each day or week. By doing so, we can build our own journal of encouragement, perhaps even to share with our own sons and daughters as they teach our grandchildren.

Cathy Duffy,
1995

ABOUT THE AUTHOR

Bobbie Howard is the wife of Michael Howard, a retired United States Air Force Security Policeman, and she is the mother of two children, Heather Lee and Matthew. During her first year of home schooling, Bobbie received her GED from Wilson High School in Washington, D.C.

Bobbie has written numerous editorials, been featured in three newspaper articles dealing with home education, had articles published in *The Teaching Home Magazine*, done a television interview for a local Portsmouth, New Hampshire, television station on home education, and received the Great American Family Community Award at the local level for 1989 and 1990 from First Ladies Nancy Reagan and Barbara Bush, and K. Wayne Scott, President of the National Family Society. These awards were presented to the Howard family by then Colonel Orin L. Godsey, Commander of Pease Air Force Base in New Hampshire.

INTRODUCTION

This devotional began in the same way most literary works begin. I had a need to express my feelings, a desire to share my experiences, and a need to be encouraged in my endeavors. It seemed to me the most natural thing to do; after all, if I needed encouragement, other mothers must need it also.

The first devotion appeared in our local Home School Newsletter. We had just become the editors, and I wanted to say something encouraging to the many new families that had begun teaching their children. By the third or fourth telephone call from excited mothers, I knew the need was there. By the third or fourth devotion, my husband began to see this as something "much bigger." Michael's enthusiasm and encouragement were contagious, and before I knew where to begin, I already had.

The next step was to mention the thought of a book to my prayer partners and see their reaction. Bonnie Marsh has prayed over every page of this devotional and over me. Constant prodding from my husband to sit down (remember, he is a husband, and he thinks mothers get to do this from time to time), and the encouragement of his prayers, gave me the vision to pen these words.

This book is the result of yielding to the Holy Spirit. Its purpose is to place our focus on the Lord and His purpose for our home schools, and to gently remind us that it is Jesus Christ who not only called us to this great work but equipped us to complete it. If the words of His Book, the Bible, and the words of my heart encourage you to carry on, then we have accomplished more than I have ever dreamed.

Gregg Harris, Mary Pride, Dr. Raymond Moore, Dr. James Dobson of Focus On The Family, and Sue Welch of *The Teaching Home* have been, and are, major influences in my life. They have the ability to reach into our spirit, find the soldier that lurks inside, and see that we have the proper equipment to fight this battle. These great pioneers have blazed a trail for us, and it is our responsibility to build on that trail, straight to the very heart of God.

This is my small contribution to this road. I hope it helps to speed you on your way and also provides you with a rest stop here and there. We have much work to do; the future belongs to God, and He wants us refreshed and battle-ready.

May God our Father direct your path, may Jesus Christ shepherd you along it and may the Holy Spirit breathe fresh vision into your heart as you climb to the top of the mountain called Home Education. God bless you!

DEDICATION

This book is dedicated to Jesus Christ, the Author and Finisher of my Faith. May He be glorified on every page and in my heart. And to my family: Michael's love and support holds me together; his prayers and leadership stitch together the fabric of my days. Heather Lee and Matthew are my blessings from God, the joy in my day and the inspiration I need; they are often my teachers. I love you all so much!

To the pioneers who have blazed the trail and worn out their shoes, to the tenderfoots that are stepping lightly on the trail, and to those who have yet to put on their shoes, this book is for you.

HOW TO USE THIS BOOK

This book is designed to give you encouragement throughout the school year. The verses may be read daily, weekly, monthly, or all at once. They can be used as beginnings of prayers to refresh your spirit or to share with others. Use this book in the way you need to at any specific time during your school year.

May you find encouragement through these pages, and God bless your endeavors to teach your children. "Let the words of my mouth and the meditation of my heart be acceptable in Your sight, O Lord, my rock and my redeemer" (Psalm 19:14).

"For My thoughts are not your thoughts; neither are your ways My ways, says the Lord. For as the heavens are higher than the earth, so are My ways higher than yours, and My thoughts than your thoughts."

—Isaiah 55:8-9

READING 1

When my husband and I decided to remove our children from the government school systems, we thought we were rescuing them from a failing academic structure with increasing persecution for their religious beliefs. Our thoughts were good. The desire sprang from love and concern for our children. Our way to accomplish this rescue was home schooling. This way came about because, financially, there was no other way. We had never met anyone who home schooled, never heard of home schooling, and we thought this decision sprang from desperation. Little did we know — God had a plan.

God's thoughts are higher than our thoughts. As we began to study the Bible, we discovered that He had planned home schooling all along. It wasn't new or creative on our part; He had placed it on our hearts, not to rescue our children from a failing academic future, but to rescue their spirits and souls from a failing world. He wasn't concerned about their grade in science; God wanted them to know the One that holds all things together.

His way is clear. God had no apprehensions — we did. He knew that parents had tender hearts toward their children and could instill in them the character that will make them men and women after God's own heart.

His way is perfect. No matter how He brought you to this place, you can be confident of this one thing: His ways and thoughts are higher than yours, and that is why He placed them in your heart of hearts.

JOURNAL

"I, the Lord, will instruct you and teach you in the way you should go; I will counsel you with My eye upon you."

—Psalm 32:8

READING 2 When the Lord revealed to us that we were to begin this great adventure known as home education, I had a wide spectrum of emotions. They ranged from joy to fear. The joyful emotion is understandable; our children had been in public school for five years, and the experience almost destroyed our family. Tears in the eyes of one or more members of the family were almost a daily occurrence.

The fear, however, caught me by surprise. In fact, I was so surprised that it took a while to pinpoint its origin. The fear was not the fear of the unknown, nor was it the fear of government authorities. The fear was a fear I had often suppressed — the fear of inadequacy. When it surfaced, this monstrosity, PANIC, gripped my heart. I had met him before on the battlefield of motherhood. Would I be a good mother? He had reared his head again, the year we contemplated divorce. Was I an adequate mate? Now in the midst of all my joyful preparations, he was back!

At first he began to whisper challenges in my ear. He whispered, " How will you teach them when you can't make them do their homework?" I ignored that thought by telling myself that now I would know what they were expected to accomplish. As I continued with my search for curricula and wrote the various satellite schools, he spoke to me a little louder: "You are sure to choose the wrong path; you know nothing about teaching." But my ever faithful Jesus chose the right path for our family.

This caused the Spirit of Fear to scream viciously at me. Much to my surprise, but in keeping with his ways, he attacked my past. You know what past I mean — the one Jesus erases when you become a new creation. Shouting wildly, he screamed, "But you never finished high school!" After I picked myself up from the floor, having been dealt a potentially lethal blow, one that could crumble the structure I had begun to erect, I returned to the floor, but this time on my knees, on my own power, and began to pray. I can still hear my Savior whispering comfort into my heart: "I will instruct you. Fear not, you of little faith."

With Jesus we began, and with Jesus we remain. How faithful is our God!

JOURNAL

_____

_____

_____

_____

"Whereas the object and purpose of our instruction and charge is love which springs from a pure heart and a good [clear] conscience and sincere [unfeigned] faith."

—1 Timothy 1:5

READING 3

Spread out before me are the tools of the trade, so to speak. I have my pen, a pad of paper, and catalogs. Praise the Lord for catalogs! Mail order has come of age in the home-school movement. The U.S. Post Office and United Parcel Service owe much to the home-schooling family. However, with so many catalogs (four years ago I only had three), it has become increasingly hard to choose the proper materials. I must choose among textbooks, workbooks, capsules, manipulatives, and time lines. Our finances tend to dictate the direction we take, as well as the "hand-me-down" ability of what we purchase. But what of content?

As I pick two from column A and one from column B, my eyes and heart stop and read 1 Timothy 1:5. How do my choices stack up to the Word of God? Will the books I've chosen encourage my children's faith-walk with God? Will they be confused by contradictory messages, or will they have a clear conscience? Am I building a firm foundation beneath their feet? And is my purpose of instruction love? For God? For them? For others? Am I able to foster a heart that seeks after God's heart? Which catalog contains the heart of God? Love that springs from a pure heart and a clear conscience can only be found in the Word of God. The Bible must take precedence in our curriculum, and our curriculum must not contradict the Scriptures.

That certainly does cause one to walk through the narrow gate of catalogs, doesn't it? May the Lord Jesus Christ direct you to His choices for your children as you seek to fulfill His plan for your family. God bless you!

JOURNAL

"The person that has my commands and keeps them is the one who [really] loves me, and whoever [really] loves me will be loved by my Father, and I [too] will love him and will show [reveal, manifest] Myself to him—I will let Myself be clearly seen by him and make Myself real to him."

—*John 14:21*

READING 4

When we first began this adventure known as home schooling, I wasn't sure how this verse would become a reality to me. The women in my morning Bible study questioned me about not teaching them next year. All I could say was that I had to put it aside for now. "What about the evening studies? You will still go to them, right?" No, not now. My family has been fragmented for too long. It is going to take some time to heal it. "Where will we find another Sunday School teacher in the fall?" I assured them that the Lord would provide. I just didn't have time to prepare properly, so I declined.

Not everyone has to give up everything else in order to teach their children. I did. I knew it would be a while before I felt confident enough to tackle anything else. All of my energies had to be directed to our home school. Instead of feeling let down by having to give up my free time, I discovered that I was blessed. The Lord began to reveal Himself to me in a more intimate and personal way than ever before. Instead of searching the Scriptures for my students and lesson plans, I began to experience them as a love letter from

Jesus to me. I began to find ways to express that love to the children, and I saw the Lord begin to reveal Himself to me in The Scriptures. The more I followed His commands, the closer I walked according to His plan, the deeper my love for Him became.

After the first year, I added an evening Bible study to my schedule — one to attend, not one to teach. I began to teach Vacation Bible School during the summer, and I added a Sunday School class later on. Five years later I began to teach a women's Bible study again. I had finally learned how to teach others and still see the Lord clearly without overextending myself.

JOURNAL

_____

_____

_____

_____

_____

_____

_____

_____

"Through skillful and godly Wisdom is a house [a life, a home, a family] built, and by understanding it is established [on sound and good foundation]. And by knowledge shall the chambers [of its every area] be filled with all precious and pleasant riches."

—*Proverbs 24:3-4*

READING 5

My father-in-law is a general contractor and is in the process of building his dream house. It is a slow, painstaking process, since he works on his home over the weekends and in the evenings, if light and weather allow.

He began building it in his heart long before the first nail was hammered into place. He is the only one with the finished picture — the only one who can see it in his heart. Although he dreams about the pictures hung in place, he knows that without a sound foundation, it would be useless to live in. The same thing applies to our children and their schooling. We have to start with a good foundation. If we don't, all that we teach, all that they learn, will crumble. If Jesus isn't the foundation we build upon, the blocks will all fall down and Humpty-Dumpty will never be put back together again.

Precious treasures can be placed in all the chambers. We can place Character in one chamber, Math in another, and Science in yet another. But the chambers won't stand up to the wind, rain, and floods which the world will send against them, unless the foundation is sound, the materials of the finest quality, and the builder skilled in his trade.

The Bible is our blueprint; the Master Builder has planned it to the finest detail; and the materials were purchased at great cost. Now we must lay the foundation and begin to build a structure that will last, no matter what shall befall it. We have but to begin.

JOURNAL

"*Blessed [happy, fortunate, prosperous, and enviable] is the man who walks and lives not in the counsel of the ungodly [following their advice, their plans, and purposes] nor stands [submissive and inactive] in the path where sinners walk, nor sits down [to relax and rest] where the scornful [and the mockers] gather.*"

—*Psalm 1:1*

READING 6

Of all the confrontations I encounter over the decision to home school, my greatest opposition comes from other Christians. If I were to say, "I want our children to have the best academics available," I am sure their opposition would not be so vocal. But since our reasoning is our complete conviction that the Word of God commands us to teach our children at home, frontal attacks are common. After all, if it is the Biblical thing to do, and they aren't doing it, then they feel that I am accusing them of not following God's Word. But all I said was, "We are, because God commands us to." They asked the question.

As I read Psalm 1, I am encouraged as to the path we have chosen to walk upon. If I sent our children to government schools, I would send a message to my children which is contrary to God's Word. I would say, "Listen to your teacher, obey your teacher's instruction, pay attention." Then I would say, "Your teacher is wrong, God created the Universe, the Bible is relevant, abortion is murder." So much for the counsel of the ungodly. Their plans and purposes are not the same as God's.

If I said, "Just sit there and ignore the classes on sexual freedom, evolution, and globalism," wouldn't I really be saying, "Stand with them, be inactive and submissive, don't rock the boat or take a stand"? If I said, "It's only a school dance — go ahead, have fun!" Wouldn't I really be saying, "Relax, rest, sit down with the mockers of God," since their music glorifies the deeds of darkness?

The ever-present argument is: "They are called to be a light to the world." I do not see it as an argument but a confirmation: "Look, World, blessed, happy, fortunate, prosperous, and enviable is the home-schooling family."

JOURNAL

_____

_____

_____

_____

_____

_____

_____

_____

_____

"So whoever cleanses himself [from what is ignoble and unclean] - who separates himself from contact with contaminating and corrupting influences—will [then himself] be a vessel set apart and useful for honorable and noble purposes, consecrated and profitable to the Master, fit and ready for any good work."

—2 Timothy 2:21

READING 7

"Socializing" is a word we are all too familiar with in home-schooling families. Government authorities have clear-cut ideas as to how this is to be accomplished; a few are even considering ways to "enforce" this process, especially in the home-schooling sector. We should not be surprised at increased governmental regulation.

However, our Father in Heaven also has His own ideas in this matter, and not surprising, either, is the contrast between God's plan and man's plan. His thoughts and ways are indeed above our thoughts and ways (see Is. 55:8-9).

Our Father wants us fit for His good work, ready to carry out His plans for our society. This is to be accomplished by separating ourselves from contaminating influences. I have had time to consider this, as I have spent the last week under the influence of a contaminating influence — a virus. Because of this impurity in my body, I have not been fit to do my Master's bidding, and any noble enterprise I was hoping to perform has been postponed.

We have plumb lines in our home for measuring such influences in our lives as television, movies, books, activities, etc. One we use most often is Phil. 4:8. If the program doesn't measure up, then it's not for us. What is your measuring stick? How are you becoming a vessel fit for the Master's use?

In closing, I would like to share this definition with you from the American Heritage Dictionary of the English Language. Pay close attention to the first meaning listed: Socialize - 1. To place under government or group ownership or control; establish a socialistic basis. 2. To fit for companionship with others; make sociable in attitude or manners. 3. To convert or adapt to the needs of society.

JOURNAL

_____

_____

_____

_____

_____

_____

_____

_____

"To make it your ambition and definitely endeavor to live quietly and peacefully, to mind your own affairs, and to work with your hands as we charged you; so that you may bear yourselves becomingly, be correct and honorable and command the respect of the outside world, being [self-supporting] dependent on nobody and having need of nothing."

—*1 Thessalonians 4:11,12*

READING 8

The Home Education Regulations in our state contain a clause for those who desire to claim religious exemption. A portion of this clause reads: "the disruption of the child's education should not seriously impair the child's future nor should it threaten the public order in any way." This clause is only addressed in the Religious Exemption portion of our regulations.

Because of this, I came to the following conclusion. First, because I am teaching our child at home, the government assumes our child's education has been forever disrupted, not enhanced. The second conclusion is that since I have disrupted his education, the only possible outcome is for our child to be a constant burden to society, doomed forever to stand in the welfare lines, or worse, to become a preacher. If this clause had been a part of the entire regulation, I might not have been so agitated, but it wasn't for everyone — just for the religious fanatics.

The Bible verse that I began this with commands us to rear up our children to be self-supporting, to work with their hands, mind their own business, and be at peace with their neighbors. If our children are dependent on anyone, they are dependent on God. If this regulation were a part of a contract between the government schools and the parents as they enrolled their children, would our nation's illiteracy rate go down? Would the welfare lines be diminished? Would the teachers and parents be willing to assure the government that the public order would in no way be threatened? Could they?

A woman at our State Board of Education meeting asked that our regulations become more restrictive. She demanded that parents who teach in the home be required to be regulated the same way the public schools are: certification, six hour days, equal curriculum, and monitoring. It seems to me that if she were truly concerned with the education and welfare of the children, she would be demanding that the government schools meet our standards and regulations, wouldn't she?

1 Thessalonians 4:11,12 may never be their ambition, but it will always be ours.

JOURNAL

_____

_____

_____

_____

"They confronted and came upon me in the day of my calamity; but the Lord was my stay and support. He brought me forth also into a large place; He was delivering me, because He was pleased with me and delighted in me."

—Psalm 18:18, 19

READING 9

We had just completed our morning prayers and Bible Study. By this time, I normally had the answering machine turned on so that our school day could progress uninterrupted. Today I had neglected to turn it on. As the phone rang, I chastised myself for being forgetful and answered the telephone. The man on the phone asked for my husband. I informed him that Mike was at work and offered to take a message. He asked if I were Mrs. Howard, and after I affirmed that, he stated that he was from the Department of Children's Social Services, and an anonymous telephone call had reported us for "Child Neglect"! My heart stopped beating; my mind kept functioning. All of the training I had gotten from Home School Legal Defense Association took over, and God graciously got me through that telephone call.

The man had lied about his knowledge of home schooling and worked very hard to entrap me. God protected me, and the Holy Spirit gave me the right words at the right time. "Thank you for your concern. I can assure you I am not neglecting my children's education. Please give me your name and telephone number, and I will have my lawyer contact you immediately." He was reluctant to do so and kept asking more questions. I told him that our lawyers would gladly enlighten him as to the home-school regulations of this state and asked him again to give me his telephone number. He finally did, and I hung up the telephone.

The next few minutes in our home were comical. I called HSLDA and the secretary said, "I am sorry, but he's in a meeting right now. I'll have him call you back right away." I called my husband at work, and his secretary said, "I'm sorry, but he's in a meeting right now. I'll have him call home as soon as he comes in." I called the children together, and we began to pray. Hallelujah! God was not in a meeting!

God answered our prayers; HSLDA called, and they straightened everything out with one telephone call, and God has been glorified many times over.

JOURNAL

_____

_____

_____

_____

_____

_____

"Let the word of Christ dwell in you richly as you teach and admonish one another with all wisdom, and as you sing psalms, hymns and spiritual songs with gratitude in your hearts to God."

—Colossians 3:16 [NIV]

READING 10

Because I am a mother teaching at home, I am pulled to this verse often. Actually it tugs at my heart strings. After all, how often do I teach and admonish our children with "all" wisdom? So often it is in my wisdom, the wisdom that our Lord calls foolishness in 1 Corinthians 1:20, instead of it being wisdom from above. On the days when I neglect to appropriate that godly wisdom, it is evident. There is a lack of understanding between the children and me. Nothing seems to "click." It is undeniable that today I am in my own strength and not the Lord Jesus' strength, and I am not using the gray matter between my ears. I struggle to gain control, and I don't know how I lost it. Then miraculously a light goes on. Actually the light is allowed to illuminate the dark hidden "me" places. All I need to do is to get a grip on His Word. It is so simple! If I just do the Word of God, everything falls into place.

If I love as 1 Corinthians 13 tells me to, if I walk as 1 John directs me to, if I follow James' advice and hold my tongue; if I do these things and sing praises to the Lord with our children, then a wondrous thing happens, with gratitude in our hearts, school is a joy!

Mind you, the children must also follow Jesus' Word to have this pleasant teaching environment. They must obey their parents because it pleases the Lord (and Mom, too!); they must do all things without grumbling and complaining as Philippians 2:14 directs them to; and if they put others' interests ahead of their own, then "great will be the peace of our children" (and Moms, too!). The fruit of this is found in 3 John 4: "I have no greater joy than to hear that my children are walking in the truth" (NIV) (and Mom too!).

JOURNAL

_____

_____

_____

_____

_____

_____

_____

_____

_____

_____

_____

"And I [now] announce to him that I will judge and punish his house forever for the iniquity of which he knew, for his sons were [blaspheming God] bringing curses upon themselves, and he did not restrain them"

—1 Samuel 3:13

READING 11

I begin my prayers in my room; the door is shut; my heart is open. Soon, I discover that I am in the Holy of Holies, offering up a sacrifice of praise to the Holy One of Israel. Sweet incense fills this place. If given the choice, I would never leave it. It would be a wondrous thing to be able to ignore the world around me and bask in the light of His love. However, I do not live in the Heavenlies yet, so I must return to earth. Some days I am brought back to earth rather rudely. No sooner do I enter this Holy Place, than my children begin quarreling in the hall. It would be easy to ignore them. If I focused hard enough on the Lord, their shouts would disappear.

I am sure Eli felt the same way I feel. After all, I am with the Lord God Almighty. What greater honor is there than lighting the incense and burning the sacrifice at His altar? Rather abruptly, I remember Eli's reward for ignoring his children, so I leap to my feet and confront them. Peace returns to our home, and I to my prayers.

All of the character-building curriculum in the world could not build our children's character as well as our examples do. When you are in prayer, on the phone, on a field trip, will you stop and restrain your children? Or will you turn a deaf ear to them as Eli did?

JOURNAL

_____

_____

_____

_____

_____

_____

_____

_____

_____

_____

_____

_____

_____

_____

_____

"Train up a child in the way he should go [and in keeping with his individual gift or bent], and when he is old he will not depart from it."

—Proverbs 22:6

READING 12

I would like to introduce you to some of my peers. They are selfish, materialistic, and lack values. I believe they are the result of a public educational system that incorporated basal reading and evolution with the dismissal of prayer and patriotism. They became a generation with an identity crisis and the coiners of the phrase: "I need to find myself."

It is from the mouths of my peers that I am often challenged on our decision to home school our children. I am told by these scholarly individuals that public education didn't hurt them at all. If it was good enough for them, it's good enough for my children. If I want to teach them Christian principles and Creationism, I can do that "after school." However, when I see the lives they lead, without direction, without godly values, I am hard-pressed to discover how their public education benefited them.

Proverbs 22:6 gives us specific instructions for rearing children. It says to train up our children, not re-train them. I have discovered time and time again that learning to do something properly the first time is simpler than having to learn how to do something right after I have learned to do it incorrectly. If I train up our children, not only will they benefit from it, but so will our nation. Some people may not agree with what we are doing, but I want to do it right the first time, and I believe this is the right way for our family.

JOURNAL

"Do all things without grumbling and fault finding and complaining [against God] and questioning and doubting [among yourselves]."

—Philippians 2:14

READING 13

It's been raining for a week straight. The children are constantly looking out the window. They wonder if Noah felt this way, too. If I step on one more forgotten building block, I'll scream! Or will I? Does this verse cover rainy days? Does it apply to days when school work drags out for hours? Where do I place the blame? The weatherman? The textbook? The three years they spent in public education? My prayer life? I keep looking for a place to put the blame, everywhere but in the mirror. I complain about the bad attitudes, cloudy skies, unfinished housework and a daydreaming child. I begin to question my abilities to teach our children. Do I need to be certified? Would a college degree really make a difference?

Who am I really doubting? Myself or God? After all, didn't He say that I can do all things through Christ? Didn't He say He would instruct me? "Lord, forgive me for doubting you, blaming you. You are God and nothing is impossible with God."

When my head begins to clear, unlike the cloudy skies outside, light gives birth to new ideas. Perhaps a board game would induce a smile on their lips. Maybe a skit would drive home the history lesson that seems to be evading them. Noah must have considered life on an ark deeply enough to know what to do on the "down" days. Perhaps they played circus with the elephants and monkeys, or perhaps they made up words to the tunes of the song birds. If the Lord could instruct Noah on the rainy days, He can instruct me also; I only have to pause and listen.

Lord, remind us often of Your promises; the rain will stop, the rainbow will delight the sky and we will find joy in the midst of today.

JOURNAL

_____

_____

_____

_____

_____

_____

_____

_____

READING 13

"I have the strength for all things in Christ who empowers me. I am ready for anything and equal to anything through Him Who infuses inner strength into me, [that is, I am self-sufficient in Christ's Sufficiency.]"

—Philippians 4:13

READING 14

I can't do it! My husband puts his arms around me, and I cry. He doesn't ask what's wrong; he knows. I have spent all day struggling with some basic mathematical concept that just isn't sinking into our child's head. "We've tried everything!" I tell him. "I just can't explain it." He hands me a tissue, strokes my hair and says, "Let me try." I hand him the book, and he works the problem just as I had. He calls in our child and calmly explains each process in the formula. Our child takes the math book and in 15 minutes completes every problem correctly.

As I watch this scene, I think of other times "I can't" has been on my lips. I remember a doctor saying, "Don't push!" I responded, "I can't!" He says, "Now push hard!" I retort, "I can't!" The next thing I know, I'm holding the most beautiful baby in the world.

I may lack faith in myself at times, but if I always keep faith in Jesus, I have great success. He has never failed me, although I have failed Him. There will be days when we feel like tossing in the towel — maybe it's just time to do the laundry. A good cleansing breath — breathe in Christ Jesus, and the victory is ours.

JOURNAL

_____

_____

_____

_____

_____

_____

_____

_____

_____

_____

_____

_____

_____

_____

_____

_____

_____

_____

_____

_____

_____

_____

_____

_____

_____

"All your children will be taught of the Lord, and great will be your children's peace."

—Isaiah 54:13 [NIV]

READING **15** Why am I teaching my children at home? I am asked this question so often, and so often I respond, "I believe it is what God has told our family to do." Other answers are: "I want them to get the best education available, and this is the best," or "They don't need to be exposed to the humanistic ideology of government schools."

There are many varied reasons for home schooling our children, yet how often do we consider the reason mentioned in Isaiah 54? "Great will be the peace of our children as they are taught in the Lord." What a precious promise from our Lord. In an age where hopelessness is the result of the teaching in government schools, what a gift to give our children.

Is Jesus' peace evident in our children? In our home? In us? What are we doing to cultivate this gift? The next time someone asks you why you are teaching your child at home, will you say, "So great will be the peace of my child"?

"Peace I leave with you. My peace I give to you. I do not give to you as the world gives. Do not let your hearts be troubled and do not be afraid."

John 14:27 (NIV)

JOURNAL

"*For with God, nothing is ever impossible, and no word from God shall be without power or impossible of fulfillment.*"

—*Luke 1:37*

READING 16

Mary, the mother of Jesus, was a young, tenderhearted woman with a desire to serve God. No one had any idea what lay ahead of her. She loved the Lord with all her heart, soul, mind, and strength as the Scriptures commanded her. She would obey the Word of the Lord, even if it would cost her everything, including her life.

As I look into the sparkling green eyes of our daughter, I can't help but wonder. Would she have believed an Angel of the Lord? Does she love the Lord enough to lay down her life? Would she be asked to do it somewhere down the line? How can parents ever be sure that their child will choose Christ over all else? I don't know.

But I do know she is ready to try. God only wants a heart that is willing, and she has that. I also know that she doesn't go alone or in her own strength. She is about the same age as the mother of our Lord was, when God called Mary into full time service. Our daughter has so many decisions ahead of her. Lord, help us to equip her for every good work.

JOURNAL

_____

_____

_____

_____

_____

_____

_____

_____

_____

_____

_____

_____

_____

_____

_____

_____

_____

_____

_____

_____

_____

_____

_____

_____

"But Jacob replied, 'You know my Lord, that the children are tender and delicate, and need gentle care, and the flocks and herds with young are of concern to me; for if the man should overdrive them for a single day, the whole of the flocks would die.'"

—Genesis 33:13

READING **17** I came across this verse a few years ago in my devotional reading. The moment I read it, my heart skipped a beat. I knew this verse applied to the adventure I had just begun — home schooling. I had no idea how much I would rely on its guidance in the days and years to come.

There are some of us whose home schooling is being monitored by our local public school administration. I am bringing this verse to your attention today because as the school year passes, the school boards will be looking for "results." Mostly, they will center on the "amount" of work accomplished, not the quality. This can cause stress for the parent as well as the child.

The verse above challenges the parent to keep our goal in mind. Our goal is not completion for completion's sake or competition with the school system. Our goal is to produce children of Godly character, with tender hearts, secure in their strengths and weaknesses, and able to retain the knowledge presented to them. The school board, like Esau, may attempt to push us on at a pace not natural to our children. It is my prayer that I might always answer as Jacob did, "What need is there for it? Let me find favor in the sight of my Lord." And let us "Be diligent to know the state of your flocks...." (Proverbs 27:23) and pace ourselves accordingly.

JOURNAL

_____

_____

_____

_____

_____

_____

_____

_____

_____

_____

_____

_____

_____

_____

"But refuse and avoid irreverent legends—profane and impure and godless fictions, mere grandmother's tales—and silly myths and express your disapproval of them. Train yourself toward godliness [piety]—keeping yourself spiritually fit."

—1 Timothy 4:7

READING 18

Teaching our children at home has caused me to look deeply into the content of the material I am to teach. Even Christian publishers might include material that is in contrast to many Biblical principles. Using the Bible as a standard to judge quality literature may cause you to comb library shelves for books to read.

When teaching our children Greek and Roman history, I thought it might be fun to read a great literary work by Homer entitled "The Odyssey." I managed to get through a page and a half. No matter how open-minded I tried to be, telling myself that it is considered to be "one of the greatest literary works of the world," I just couldn't read it. Every time I spoke the words "King of Kings" in reference to a mythological god, the words stuck in my throat. How could I read anything that called anyone other than Jesus Christ, "King of Kings"?

Some say our standards are too high; I just reply, "God's standards are much higher." Training our children and ourselves toward godliness isn't easy; neither is following Jesus. No matter what the cost, we will follow Jesus. How about you?

JOURNAL

_____

_____

_____

_____

_____

_____

_____

_____

_____

_____

_____

_____

_____

_____

_____

_____

_____

_____

_____

_____

_____

_____

_____

"Whoever loves discipline loves knowledge, but he who hates correction is stupid."

—*Proverbs 12:1*

READING **19** When our son Matthew attended government schools, he learned to hate correction. If he had a problem wrong in class, he was laughed at and ridiculed. To ask a question was to be labeled "stupid", contrary to God's Word. God delights in our questions. They are not too difficult for Him to answer. Jesus' blood was shed to erase our mistakes. He would never laugh at them or ridicule us.

I would love to say that home schooling has healed all these hurt places in his heart, but it hasn't—not yet. He still hates to be wrong; however, he is learning to love knowledge. He has also been taught that not knowing the answer in most instances is either because he is too anxious to complete his work, or he has something new to learn and needs assistance. Asking for assistance doesn't come very easy to him. I must be more vigilant in seeking out opportunities to assist him in asking for assistance. Questions like 'Are my instructions understandable?' or 'How would you suggest we tackle this assignment?' open doors in a non-threatening manner. Doors are opening and slowly wounds are closing.

"Disciple" and "discipline" have the same root word. If we are to make disciples out of our children, we must first be an example to them in this area ourselves. They need to watch us carefully read all the instructions before we begin assembling a new toy. They need to be with us when we ask for assistance or directions. They must learn to embrace discipline, not just run from it. Accepting correction with the proper attitude is something we should all practice. The benefits will be worth the efforts.

JOURNAL

"No unbelief or distrust made him waver or doubtingly question concerning the promise of God, but he grew in faith as he gave praise and glory to God, fully satisfied and assured that God was able and mighty to keep His Word and to do what he had promised."

—Romans 4:20, 21

READING **20** A friend called me the other day in tears. She just didn't know if she could continue teaching her child at home. It seemed her daughter just didn't respond to the methods she was using. All the latest "how to's" only brought her more confusion. She began to waver and doubt her abilities and her God. In talking with her, I just knew I had to come up with a pearl of wisdom to bring about the change necessary in her situation. I struggled, looking for the right words. But nothing, absolutely nothing came out that seemed inspired. After we hung up, I went away to pray. As I began to pray for her family, praise and thanksgiving rose up within me. A flood of praises came out of my mouth and heart concerning the growth of this family's faith. I had seen such a change in the hearts of the mother, the daughter, and the father. God was knitting them so closely together.

Then it hit me like a bolt of lightning. I don't have to possess all the answers; I belong to the Almighty God, Maker of heaven and earth. He knows all the questions and all the answers. All I have to do is to be fully satisfied that

God will do as He promises. When I called her back, the momentary crisis had passed, and peace had been restored to her home and heart once more.

JOURNAL

_____

_____

_____

_____

_____

_____

_____

_____

_____

_____

_____

_____

_____

_____

_____

_____

_____

_____

"But the Lord said to me, 'Say not
I am only a youth; for you shall
go to all to whom I shall send you
and whatever I command you,
you shall speak. Be not afraid of
them [their faces] for I am with you
to deliver you,' says the Lord."

–Jeremiah 1:7,8

READING 21

I watch the teenagers that live in our neighborhood going through life aimlessly. A dense fog surrounds them; depression follows them. These precious young people, a blessing from God, are lonely and hopeless. A whole generation has grown up in fear.

As I sit across from my teenager, I look into her eyes and see a peace that can only come through knowing Christ as her Savior. The joy of the Lord truly is a strength in her life. She does not fear her future; she knows it is in God's hands. His Word tells her that He desires only goodness and mercy to follow her all the days of her life, and that there is no fear in love. She is deeply loved.

Often I catch myself saying, "She is only a youth." How can one so young affect the world for Christ? Then I see her sharing Jesus with a friend whose parents are divorcing, and I know God does indeed send out the youth to speak His words to a lost generation.

Parents, I want to encourage you. I want you to see how God's hand is moving across our land, as home after home returns to God and His commands. We are helping to raise up a generation of godly men and women who are going to be the leaders of tomorrow; a generation that will speak the words God has given them to speak, without fear; a generation that speaks even now in its youth.

JOURNAL

_____

_____

_____

_____

_____

_____

_____

_____

_____

_____

_____

_____

_____

_____

_____

_____

"Let no one delude and deceive you with empty excuses and groundless arguments [for these sins], for through these things the wrath of God comes upon the sons of rebellion and disobedience."

—Ephesians 5:6

READING 22 When our daughter entered sixth grade, I began to search our public library for information on menstruation. Something straight-forward and simple to understand was all I was looking to find. What I found was a book whose cover said, "For Mothers & Daughters." The suggested reader's age began at eight years old. I checked out this book and took it home. What I read in those pages shocked me. There was a list of immoral, disgusting slang terms for the reproductive parts of the human body. It suggested that one out of ten children is homosexual and should be encouraged to experiment. This book was written by a public school teacher entrusted with the care of shaping and directing children's minds. In this case the direction leads to the heartache of immorality. The book used one excuse after another to support its godless ideas. It repeatedly tried to convince the reader to accept ideas contrary to the Word of God.

Eventually I turned to our encyclopedia for visual aid and my Bible for direction. We had a great discussion. She learned all about the amazing way God designed her body, and I didn't have to use slang, once. Instead she learned that she is fearfully and wonderfully made.

JOURNAL

"See to it that no one carries you off as spoil or makes you yourselves captive by his so-called philosophy and intellectualism, and vain deceit [idle fancies and plain nonsense] following human tradition - men's ideas of the material [rather than the spiritual] world—just crude notions following the rudimentary and elementary teachings of the universe, and disregarding [the teachings of] Christ the Messiah."

—Colossians 2:8

READING 23

History books constantly attempt to teach history without teaching (or even mentioning) God's plan for man, the fulfilled prophecies, the fallen kingdoms, and the birth of Jesus Christ. It is history without the Historian. Science, in its evolutionary intellectualism, reduces the beginning of man to a chance happening. That causes man to be without direction, coming from nothing, going nowhere. In choosing your textbooks, see to it that your children are not carried off as spoil in the battle for their hearts and mind. Examine your textbooks carefully with a critical eye. The very souls of your children are at stake. Aren't they worth protecting?

Christ paid dearly for our redemption. Is it asking too much of us to see to it that Christ is not disregarded in our textbooks? I think not.

JOURNAL

_____

_____

_____

_____

_____

_____

_____

_____

_____

_____

_____

_____

_____

_____

_____

_____

_____

_____

_____

_____

_____

"Moreover your little ones whom you said would become a prey, and your children, who at this time cannot discern between good and evil, they shall enter Canaan, and to them I will give it, and they shall possess it."

—Deuteronomy 1:39

READING 24

Can you imagine what it would be like to be with Moses as the Lord parts the Red Sea, pours manna from Heaven, gives you water from a rock, and heals your body from the bites of fiery serpents, only to stand in an assembly and be told you cannot enter into the Promised Land? How relieved they must have been to know that their children would not only enter Canaan but possess it! Every parent wants his child's life to be better than his own. So when God commanded parents to diligently teach their children His commands, they did it! I am sure that many of them felt deprived and even grumbled and complained about it. I am also sure that we have done the same thing and know others that still do. You know what I mean; things like: "If only I hadn't gone to public school;" " Private schools teach God in them, so they must be good substitutes for public schools," or "If we paid the teachers more, they would do a better job." Yet we are given the opportunity to give Canaan to our children. We can teach them at home as God has said, so that they will learn to discern good from evil.

I can't count how many times I have heard parents say, "I have taught Creation to my children; they know the truth," only to turn to their children and say, "Those teachers are being paid by my tax dollars to teach you something, so you had better listen and listen good!" God says to train up our children, not to re-train them. To expect our children to be able to discern what they are supposed to believe and what is in error, is to expect more of them than God does!

When I learned how to crochet, I taught myself. I designed a suitable way to hold the yarn, and to this day, that is how I hold it. Many people have tried to teach me how to hold it the proper way, but that isn't how I learned to do it at first. The first way is comfortable; the proper way is not. I'm sure that if I practiced hard enough, I could change my style. I'm equally sure that if I constantly went over our children's textbooks and pointed out the places where they disagree with the Scriptures, I could possibly make an impression. However, if I teach them the Scriptures in our home from the start, how much more pressure will the world have to exert on them in order to change their minds, once they enter the land that is spread out before them? And they will enter the land. The only question left is, "How have they been equipped?"

JOURNAL

"Therefore He is able also to save to the uttermost—completely, perfectly, finally, and for all time and eternity—those who come to God through Him, since He is always living to make petition with God and intercede with Him and intervene for them."

—Hebrews 7:25

READING 25

On our knees, my husband and I pray for our children. Thanking God for each one, we ask Him to pour out His Spirit upon them. They are living in a generation where it is increasingly difficult to share their faith. They will need boldness if they are to bring the Truth to their friends.

As we prayed, I became aware of the fact that Jesus, too, was praying. He reminds the Father of His great sacrifice — the one that paid for us. He asks His Father, "Will they be the faithful ones walking the earth when I return?" In the same way, Mike and I pray that our children will remain in the way of the Lord and stay on the narrow path.

As we pray, as Jesus prays, we are reminded that He is able, and we find rest. The One who was able to endure the Cross, break the chains of death, raise the dead, and send the Comforter, is able to do more than we ask or dream.

Together we agree, Mike, Jesus, and me.

Amen.

JOURNAL

_____

_____

_____

_____

_____

_____

_____

_____

_____

_____

_____

_____

_____

_____

_____

_____

_____

_____

_____

_____

_____

_____

"But we look for new heavens and a new earth according to His promise, in which righteousness [uprightness, freedom from sin, and right standing with God] is to abide."

—2 Peter 3:13

READING 26

During a geography lesson at our own kitchen table, I suddenly became aware of the need not only to acquaint our children with our present earth, its states, countries, and capitols, but also to acquaint them with another earth. This new earth is being fashioned in order for them to abide with God. You can imagine their joy when we began talking about living in mansions of transparent gold, ruling nations, and walking down the riverbank with Jesus by our side. We spoke about the responsibilities of leadership and what our lives must be like in order to live in see-through houses. We decided that we didn't measure up to that one yet, but that someday we would.

After the globe was put on the shelf and math books replaced it, I watched our children and wondered to myself, "Would we have had this conversation if they were still going away to school?" I don't think so. Homework would have kept them too busy to "daydream" in the middle of a geography lesson.

JOURNAL

"He who walks [as a companion] with wise men shall be wise, but he who associates with self-confident fools will [be a fool himself and] shall smart for it."

—Proverbs 13:20

READING 27

As I check my list of friends, I find that all of them have something in common with me. We have the same interests or something that draws us to each other. Christ is the foundation of my dearest friendships. It is Christ's presence that makes these friendships eternal. I know that I can expose my heart to these friends, and it won't be stomped on. When I am with them, I am challenged, renewed, uplifted, encouraged, even molded. I pray that they are also. Because of my friends, I grow wise. If this is true for an adult, how much more is it true for our children?

I have many acquaintances — people I have met as neighbors or people from my husband's job. They are just people I know. Most of these people are not Christians; we have very little in common, and conversation is strained. I don't associate with these people except at office parties or Tupperware parties. Beyond the superficial amenities, there is no depth.

How often can you tell who your child has been playing with by the attitude he brings home? A companion of fools is a fool! So who is this fool? The Psalms say, "A fool has said in his heart there is no God." Proverbs 15:5 and 18:6 say that the fool despises his father's instructions, his lips bring contention, and his mouth invites a beating. When these attitudes show up in our home, I know our child has been in the company of fools. The opposite is true when his playmate is a wise playmate: our child is refreshed.

Are we teaching our children to choose correctly? Are they playing with wise companions? Is the Lord Jesus invited to be present in all our gatherings? I pray He plays with your children.

JOURNAL

"He who spares his rod [of discipline] hates his son, but he who loves him diligently disciplines and punishes him early."

—Proverbs 13:24

READING 28

A woman was talking to me the other day. During our conversation, she ignored her children's arguments and turned a deaf ear to their tantrums; if she did acknowledge them at all, it was with an empty threat. She mentioned more than a few times that she could never teach her "monsters" at home. "Summer was bad enough, and they never do anything I ask," she said. Obviously she didn't begin her discipline training when they were younger. I don't believe it is ever too late to start, but I do believe it will be twice as hard and take twice as long if we don't begin training early. To say she hates her children is a very strong statement, but the adjectives she uses to describe them would lead one to believe that it is possible. She belittles them, says things like, "He's such a brat!" within their earshot, and never praises their achievements.

Home schooling is not for everyone; not because there are better choices, but because not everyone is willing to make it work or is committed to following God's instructions. If a grown, responsible adult cannot get a child to pick up his toys, he won't be able to get him to study his math facts.

God says that if I love my child, I will begin his discipline early. Maybe this is because the challenges are smaller, or maybe it's because children learn over time, and we need all the time we can get. Whatever it is, it is God's Word, and The Word works! So I will follow it, and He will watch over His Word to perform it.

JOURNAL

"*And this I pray, that your love may abound yet more and more and extend to its fullest development in knowledge and all keen insight that is, that your love may [display itself in] greater depth of acquaintance and more comprehensive discernment: So that you may surely learn to sense what is vital and approve and prize what is excellent and of real value — recognizing the highest and the best, and distinguishing the moral differences.*"

—*Philippians 1:9,10*

READING 29 Conversations about home education come up in the strangest places with complete strangers. Today it happened at our children's swimming lessons. I don't know how these conversations begin, but somehow I wind up saying, "Oh, I home school our children." After the basic "Why would you want to?" questions, I always seem to have a skeptic in the crowd that gathers. This skeptic asks for my credentials, of which I have none, except for a promise from the Lord that He will instruct me. The skeptic continues with arguments about "professionals" being the only ones who can properly educate. After I refute the endless questions with evidence contrary to her thinking, she pulls out her heavy artillery and asks, "What will you do about calculus and trigonometry?" She asks this question as if these are something that every child learns, much like one learns their ABC's. Does she really believe calculus is a prerequisite for graduation? After I explain to her that many biology teachers are P.E. majors with a curriculum guide and an answer book, the same tools that home-schooling parents possess, she shakes her head and mumbles while moving away, saying, "I'm sure they are missing out on something."

Maybe our children are missing out on a few things: drugs, peer pressure, and assault. But even if they are missing out on some things, they have cornered the market on other things. They know what is vital: a personal relationship with Jesus Christ, how to prize excellence in their spiritual, emotional, and academic experiences, and how to recognize what is best and of highest moral character, thus making them valuable citizens of this nation.

Some people will never accept what we are doing, but some people also won't accept Jesus as their Savior, no matter what evidence we offer them. All in all, it is their loss.

JOURNAL

"Let everything you do be done in love [true love to God and man as inspired by God's love for us]."

—1 Corinthians 16:14

READING 30

Let everything be done in love? Even the laundry? What about mopping the floor or teaching spelling? Does it really say "in love"? Does that mean the first time I try it or every time I try it? It is so hard to be loving when your six-year-old decides that writing today's date is not what he wants to do. It only takes a minute, and he has done it a hundred times before now. Yet, for some unknown reason, today is the day he decides to be difficult.

It is so hard to be loving when things are difficult. Just ask Jesus. He knows better than anyone. After all, stiff-necked sinners, grumbling for food and water in a wilderness, are hardly lovable. Yet He loved them all. Somehow God always manages to love us anyway. This isn't to say that God won't discipline our rebellion, nor does it mean that we should overlook the rebellion of our children. What it does mean is that we should do everything in love, with the right attitude—from laundry to writing the date. If we manage to smile as we mop the floor, maybe our children will learn to smile as they write their spelling words. Maybe if we practice walking in love, our children will want to keep in step. It certainly is worth the effort.

JOURNAL

"Listen to my instruction and be wise; do not ignore it."

—*Proverbs 8:33*

READING 31 One of my greatest get-away places is the mall! I am not a "shop-a-holic," and I usually buy just a cup of tea in order to relax and chat with a friend. I enjoy watching people and looking in the shop windows. For me, it is refreshing.

As I watch the people hustle through the mall, I notice that it does not refresh others as it does me. Their pace is almost comical. One scene always occurs in front of me. A young child of four or five sits down on the ground and refuses to move. The mother threatens, counts to three, attempts walking away, but never confronts. She also frequently looks around her and makes a joke out of her child's behavior.

These children have learned to ignore instruction. They will ignore their parents, teachers, and authorities. They will ignore rules and laws. They will not listen to God's call on their lives. They will reject God, just as they have rejected their parents, unless they are confronted by their parents and taught to listen.

Listening is more than just hearing what is being said; it is responding to what is heard. Wisdom is the result of responding properly. A Bible teacher of mine once told me that the proper response to "Will you please bring me the baby's diaper?" is: "Cheerfully I will do what you ask me to do, quickly, because I love you!" It's hard to be sassy with a line like this one. It is also difficult to say "cheerfully" without a smile on your face.

JOURNAL

_____

_____

_____

_____

_____

_____

_____

_____

_____

_____

_____

_____

_____

_____

_____

_____

"Therefore do not be vague and thoughtless and foolish, but understanding and firmly grasping what the will of the Lord is."

—Ephesians 5:17

READING 32 At our women's Bible Study, we begin with prayer. Sometimes prayer lasts longer than the lesson. After praying for a particular need, I was asked, "How can you be sure the answer won't be 'no'?" I gave the matter some thought (and a quick prayer) and said, "Because it lines up with God's will, I can be sure God will do it." In His time, in His way, the Lord will answer our prayers. Our attitude needs to be one of expectancy and gratitude. These are attitudes the Lord Jesus looks for in us, and we should model, and look for in our children.

Very seldom do we give much thought to our prayers, and usually it is just long enough to formulate a sentence. If we search the Scriptures and find out what God says concerning our need, then when we pray, we know that we have our requests (1 John 5:15). How many times have we prayed "God's will be done," only to realize that we don't even have a clue as to what that might be? Is this understanding and firmly grasping what the Lord's will is? I think not. It seems more like taking a shopping list to the grocer than a petition to the King of kings. Queen Esther gave much thought and prayer over the petition she was to present to Xerxes. Presenting her petition was presenting herself as a living sacrifice; this petition could cost her her life.

Not all of our prayers are as desperate as Queen Esther's, but they all cost our Savior His life's blood. If it mattered that dearly to Jesus, should we perhaps give our prayer life a little deeper consideration than we do? If Jesus was willing to sacrifice everything in order to bridge the gap between the Father and ourselves, searching the Scriptures in order to discover God's perfect will for our lives is not asking too much of us.

Are you teaching your children how to pray? Are they recognizing the Lord's answer when it comes? If the prayer is in agreement with God's Word, it is in agreement with God's will, and a prayer worth praying.

JOURNAL

_____

_____

_____

_____

_____

"For this reason, adding your diligence [to the divine promises] employ every effort in exercising your faith to develop virtue [excellence, resolution, Christian energy]; and in [exercising] virtue, [develop] knowledge, and in [exercising] knowledge [develop] self-control, and in [exercising] self-control [develop] steadfastness [patience, endurance], and in [exercising] steadfastness [develop] godliness (piety), and in [exercising] godliness [develop] brotherly affection, and in [exercising] brotherly affection [develop] Christian love. For as these qualities are yours and increasingly abound in you, they will keep [you] from being idle or unfruitful unto the full personal knowledge of Our Lord Jesus Christ, the Messiah, the Anointed One."

—2 Peter 1:5-8

READING 33 This is to be our goal. We are to "employ every effort", and that means bringing godly teaching to our children. It says "every effort", not just Sunday School or even daily devotions. Every effort means just that: exercising our faith. Our founding fathers knew this Scripture, and that is why we clearly read: "...and the free exercise thereof," in the First Amendment to the Constitution. When the free exercise of our faith is taken away, how can we continue in an atmosphere which is clearly in direct contrast to the Word of God? We must employ every effort in exercising our faith, and that may mean bringing our children home to an atmosphere in which they are free to do just that. The results will be in their development and ours, as we put our Christian energy to work, fleeing from mediocrity. The building blocks will begin to take shape as we place one above the other. Do you see His plan? Employing every effort does put some of the responsibility on us, but this should never be confused with our need for Grace. It is by Grace that we are saved and empowered to do the work set before us. How we set about accomplishing the work set before us is what separates us from mediocrity to excellence. The work of the Holy Spirit in us causes us to desire to do all things as unto the Lord and ultimately to be conformed into His image, which is our goal.

Just getting the work done becomes striving for excellence, which brings true knowledge. By using this knowledge we develop self-control. Have you ever noticed how "at peace" the man with the answer is? He is in control and must only persevere.

Perseverance comes naturally when we work for excellence, possess the knowledge and have self-control. It is stick-to-itiveness that brings godliness. Anyone can quit, but if we hold out to the end, godliness is sure to be the result. Notice that the Lord did not say stubbornness!

Brotherly affection and Christian love are certain to be in the company of godliness. Is there a greater plan? No wonder we are told to be diligent. Look at the finished product! These are not the qualities of the idle, unfruitful, or lazy. Only the diligent, those employing every effort, will reap this harvest.

JOURNAL

"Hope deferred makes the heart sick, but when desire is fulfilled, it is a tree of life."

—*Proverbs 13:12*

READING 34

Parents, psychologists, and teenagers are alarmed at the present rate of teenage suicide. They blame television, peers, and drugs as the reasons for this increase in loss of life. Although these things do influence us daily, they are only symptoms, not the disease.

We have managed in a single generation to rob our children of the precious gift of hope. The very substance that faith is built on has been sucked out of their lives. No longer are they taught about the hope of heaven, a coming King, or the love of God. Instead they are bombarded with nuclear holocaust, AIDS, Post Abortion Syndrome, and evolution. For man, all seems hopeless in the eyes of public school children. They do not see any way to save their planet, nor any reason to try to save it. Their hope has been deferred; they're heartsick, and they are killing themselves.

What are you doing to give the gifts of hope and faith to your children? Do they know that Jesus is returning? Are they assured of their place in heaven? Is Christ Jesus their Lord and Savior? Have they tasted the fruit from the tree of life? Have you?

Jesus says to believe on Him, and you and your household will be saved. A precious promise for a precious generation.

JOURNAL

"For Adam also and for his wife the Lord God made long coats [tunics] of skins and clothed them."

—Genesis 3:21

READING 35

My husband does not like to go shopping. So, when he came home from work and announced that we were going to the mall, I was surprised. When he said that just the two of us were going, I was flabbergasted, but ready to go in seconds!

As we drove to the mall, I considered feeling his forehead to see if he had a fever. I decided against it; after all, I was on my way to the mall with my husband! He started to explain the reason for this spontaneous shopping spree, as we drove down the road. We were going to buy a jacket for Heather. Not just any jacket — we were looking for a high school jacket!

Our friends were always trying to find reasons for sending children to high school: reasons like Senior Proms, high school rings, and high school jackets. We had always determined that our children would never regret being home instead of in a government school. If they wanted a graduation celebration, we would have one. If they wanted to have school colors, we would pick them, and if Heather wanted a high school jacket, we would find one. Mike decided to surprise her with one tonight, and he wasn't going home without it.

Football jackets were everywhere. We had to find a green one, and if it had silver too, it would be perfect.

Green and silver were the school colors for Genesis High School. She chose them for her high school because green was the color of new life, creation, the born-again Christian; and silver was to symbolize Jesus, the light of the world, and herself, a city on a hill all lit up. Her high school motto is: 'In the beginning...was school at home.' So Mike was determined to find a green jacket.

For two hours we searched every sporting goods store, every department store, and every place in between. If we found a green jacket, it had a team logo already on it. We had one last store to visit, and if it wasn't there, we would go home empty-handed. We stopped at the benches just before the entrance, sat down and began to pray. Mike asked the Lord to help him find just the right jacket. As a father, he knows how important it is to give good things to his children, just because he wants to bless them. We stood up and walked inside.

We walked straight to it. It could have had lights blinking all around it, it was so obvious. Hanging on a 50% off rack was a beautiful green suede jacket. It was perfect! At the counter they took off another 10%. The Lord wanted to make sure we knew He was in on this, too! We took it to the cart in the mall that does embroidery on anything while you wait. Using platinum thread (the closest to silver), they created a one-of-a-kind masterpiece.

Heather was so excited that she cried. Mike was so happy that he didn't even mention the three hours and thirty minutes he spent at the mall without having supper. And I was thankful that the Lord really is turning the hearts of the fathers to their children in the last days.

A leather high school jacket for Genesis High School. It seems fitting, doesn't it?

Journal

"*Fathers, do not irritate and provoke your children to anger—do not exasperate them to resentment—but rear them [tenderly] in the training and discipline and the counsel and admonition of the Lord.*"

—*Ephesians 6:4*

READING 36 To teach something to your children will take time, to train them will take time, and discipline takes more time than we care to admit. I can do the dishes after dinner in about ten minutes. Heather does them in about thirty minutes, and Matthew has been known to stand at the sink for at least an hour. It would be easier to do them myself. It would be easier to use paper plates. But easier isn't always best.

Cutting the grass and trimming the yard can be easily done on a Saturday afternoon. Mike could work all week and spend a couple of hours working in the yard. When our children were small, we had to do these things all the time, plus watch the children.

It was easy for us to feel exasperated over milk rings at the bottom of "already washed" glasses and to be angry when the lawn mower cut down my tomato plants. If we mulled over things long enough, we could be resentful.

Even though moments have caused us to be irritated, we have to remember to keep our training to just that— training, not perfection. Perfection will come. Even if that means doing it again and again together at first and then on their own once the training is complete. Our responsibility is to train them to do the task set before them correctly the first time, as unto the Lord.

It has been a long time since my tomatoes have been ravaged by lawn mower blades, and a long time since our Saturdays were spent on yard work instead of family outings. Now the yard is cut during the week while Mike is at work, and glasses are checked in the rinsing process to make sure that the milk ring has been washed out. Diligence is paying off, and our children know we are pleased with their progress.

JOURNAL

_____

_____

_____

_____

_____

_____

_____

_____

"The sower sows the Word. And those that were sown on good [well adapted] soil are the ones that hear the Word, and receive and accept and welcome it and bear fruit, some thirty times as much as was sown, some sixty times as much, and some [even] a hundred times as much."

—Mark 4:14-20

READING 37 Sometimes our zeal in home schooling becomes a springboard. We desire to launch every household into our arena of blessing. In doing so, we neglect the role of our Father in preparing the ground. The results can be disastrous, if we aren't careful.

In Jesus' parable of the Sower, Jesus tells us what happens when the ground is not properly prepared. He uses four examples of the ground, which represents the hearts of men. Although it is God's will that every man be saved, not every heart is open to the Gospel. So it is with home education. Home education is God's design, but not every home is prepared to do it.

The first time this sower shares home schooling with a neighbor, the seed falls on the path to be eaten by birds. I see this person as the one who says, "What a great idea!" as he enrolls his child in the first preschool with an opening. The seed never began to grow.

When the seed is sown on stony ground, something happens to the seed. It begins to grow and grows quickly. This person loves the idea of home schooling. Joyfully she borrows your catalogs, visits your school and thinks, "This is easy; no car pools, no lunches to pack, what a breeze," only to be rudely awakened by the knock of reality. Home schooling takes commitment, and she does not have time to be so committed. It's easy to forget school this week and visit friends instead. So she says, "It's not working for me; I am sending them to school."

The third type of soil we come across is full of thorns and weeds. Thorns and weeds come in various shapes and sizes. Cares and anxieties can look like school board members ready to give you a good shaking, or they can come in the form of inadequacy, saying, "You don't have the necessary qualifications." The thorns of distraction and pleasure can be the Ladies Bible Study you wish to attend and the cup of coffee with the neighbors. These thorns can also be a desire to sleep until noon or the desire for a second income. All of a sudden you may find yourself choking on self-pity and suffocating for lack of self-fulfillment.

The fourth type of soil is the kind we need to be watchful for in order to reap a harvest. These people are out there. God has diligently prepared their hearts. They are searching for the answer, no matter what the cost. They accept the challenge and welcome with joy all that will come with this decision. They have counted the cost, prayerfully considered the demands it will make, and they develop a conviction about home schooling. They will not turn back. The roots are strong, the plant is healthy, and the fruit is sweet. It is my greatest joy to watch this seed grow.

JOURNAL

"*Your words were found, and I ate them, and Your word was to me a joy and the rejoicing of my heart; for I am called by Your name, O Lord God of hosts.*"

–Jeremiah 15:16

READING 38

The decision to bring our children home did not begin as a Christ-centered, Biblical decision, even though the Lord had laid it on our hearts. It started as a last-straw survival move, hoping to save our family and bring Christian education into our children's lives.

I have always been the kind of person to research everything, but I didn't know anyone who was home schooling. I was finally given a few addresses from my girl friend's Bible Study teacher. She was living in a hostile state and teaching underground, so all I got from her were addresses. So I pulled out my Bible and began to search for God's heart in home education.

I was so hungry. I ate my fill, digested it, ate some more, and it became a joy to me. God's Word is so explicit. Why hadn't I seen it before? No matter, now I am rejoicing! Now it is a conviction in my heart, in some ways as strong as salvation is to me. I know it is God's plan for my family. After looking into the pages of my Bible, I have found that only Jesus satisfies my soul. And only home schooling allows us to be the family I know God wants us to be. Home schooling creates a whole family: developing our character, strengthening our relationships, and teaching the whole counsel of God to all of us, not just the children.

Called by His name, we are rejoicing and truly satisfied in the comfort of His Word and our home.

JOURNAL

_____

_____

_____

_____

_____

_____

_____

_____

_____

_____

_____

_____

_____

_____

"Bid the older women similarly to be reverent and devout in their deportment, as becomes those engaged in sacred service, not slanderers or slaves to drink. They are to give good counsel and be teachers of what is right and noble, so that they will wisely train the younger women to be sane and sober-minded—temperate, disciplined—and to love their husbands and their children."

—Titus 2:3-4

READING 39

READING **39** I hadn't given much thought to my role as an "older woman"; after all, I am in my early thirties. I guess that is why I am so surprised when mothers of small children ask me for advice. I have teenagers now, but we, the other mothers and I, are the same age. I guess experience makes one an older woman, not age.

I never understood the end of the verse where it says to teach women to love their children. I thought motherhood came naturally, until I became a mother. The Lord in His mercy sent me a Christian mother to do just that very thing. How grateful I am to her and to her tenacity to share the Gospel of Jesus Christ with me. Because of Jesus' love for me, I can love others, including my children.

I hear our culture speak in the mouths of moms with toddlers, more often than I hear the Word of God. In order to "feel" vital, people believe they must leave the home and make an income. What they are really saying is, "I need a break, a meaningful conversation with an adult, and encouragement to go on." Doesn't everybody? I know I do.

However, I don't have to abandon my family. I just need an older, more experienced woman in my life to prove to me that what I am doing is not only the most rewarding experience I could have, but that it's over all too soon, and before long our children will have children of their own. Older women teach us to treasure this time and in turn to love our children at home.

JOURNAL

"Every Scripture is God-breathed—given by His inspiration—and profitable for instruction, for reproof and conviction of sin, for correction of error and discipline in obedience and for training in righteousness [that is, in holy living, in conformity to God's will in thought, purpose, and action], so that the man of God may be complete and proficient, well-fitted and thoroughly equipped for every good work."

—2 Timothy 3:16-17

READING 40

If you are looking for the secret to successful home schooling, this is it. The Word of God is the answer to successful home education. It contains all that a man of God needs to be complete. It is profitable for the teacher and the student. The Bible deserves first place in our home schools.

In our home, we begin each day with prayer and Bible study. If we don't, the Scripture rightly convicts us of sin. Yes, I said sin! James 4:17 reminds me that if I know what is right to do, and I don't do it, that is sin. However, our lives are not bound up by legalism; God's grace is sufficient to cover any sin. And by his grace we are becoming more consistent.

It is not a chore to spend this time with Jesus. We are honored to be able to enter into His presence, although some days we feel it more than others. I have tried to impart this to our children; I believe I have when I hear them pray. The Bible is not our only textbook, but it is God's great light to illuminate all textbooks. Above all the hopes and dreams we have for our children is this goal: our children will be equipped for every good work. Any textbook we choose should help them reach that goal.

JOURNAL

"And let us not get tired of doing what is right, for after a while we will reap a harvest of blessing if we don't get discouraged and give up."

—Galatians 6:9 (TLB)

READING 41

The countdown has begun; the school year is coming to a close. Have we really managed to have 180 days of "required" schooling? 180 days. In September it seemed so astronomical; yet today as the count is 150 days of completed educational experiences, I wonder where they all went. So many questions begin to arise. Did I accomplish most of the goals I had listed in September? I know I had "larger-than-life" expectations. So I am content with accomplishing most of our goals. Did the children do well on their standardized tests? Funny, I still feel the pressure of wanting to "prove" to the bureaucrats the quality of home education, even though in my heart I know we have grown more than mere academics tests can measure. Is it worth it? This is the question I mull over the most; not because I don't know the answer, but because I do. How do I measure the joy in my heart when I see a lesson learned come to life in my child's eyes, in comparison to a lesson plan book? Do the mornings when we feel as if the presence of God is hovering over our kitchen classroom, as my children bring the sins of the world and their own into the throne room, compare to the tears that are shed in frustration over a math problem that can't solve itself? How can I possibly think that a few hours of peace and quiet achieved by hustling the children off to a public school could be a worthy exchange for the spontaneous outburst of laughter that can bring us all to tears in the middle of a science lesson? Is it worth it? Yes! Yes! Yes! The blessings far outnumber the sacrifices! However, I can't help but wonder, as I look over next year's curriculum, if I'm not already walking in the "Harvest of Blessing" I am promised in Galatians 6:9. Will I be able to stand it when the flood gates open and the blessing is poured out?

JOURNAL

_____

_____

_____

_____

_____

_____

_____

"Hear, O' Israel: The Lord our God is one Lord—The only Lord. And you shall love the Lord your God with all your mind and heart and with your entire being, and with all your might. And these words, which I am commanding you this day, shall be [first] in your own mind and heart; [then] you shall whet and sharpen them as to make them penetrate and teach and impress them diligently upon the [minds and] hearts of your children, and shall talk of them when you sit in your house and when you walk by the way and when you lie down and when you rise up."

— Deuteronomy 6:4-7

READING 42

Deuteronomy 6:4-7 has been the cry of the home-schooling movement. "Teach your children all through the day." I hear these verses used to support home schooling, more than any other verses, except maybe "Train up your child..." However, upon closer examination, after all, God examines the hearts of men, so examination must be a godly characteristic; I have discovered a fault in my teaching.

Somewhere along the road between Deuteronomy 6:4 and Deuteronomy 6:7, I had made a wrong turn. You see, I had become so absorbed in diligently teaching my children ("here is your book, paper, and pencil; read chapter 10 and answer the questions"), that I misplaced (under all the papers to correct) verse 6! I'm not sure where or when, or even to what extent, I had lost it. I only know that on closer examination of my heart, I hadn't tended to my needs as well as I should have. Although we had our daily Bible Study and our prayer time, it had become a requirement, no longer did we read it as a heart-felt letter love from my Bridegroom. Was I indeed teaching our children what was first in my heart and mind? Maybe, but then again, maybe not!

The cry of my heart had not been very visible to my children because the cry of my mouth had become just do it and get it over with. My heart longed to show them the depth of the love Jesus was extending to them. I wanted to teach them to embrace the Word of God as the love letter it is intended to be. Only now I see that perhaps my own heart had turned our Bible into mere academics.

However, the Lord is faithful and causes me to pause and examine myself and in doing so, I can hear the voice of the Holy Spirit speaking ever so gently. Drink deeply from the Living Waters that refresh your soul. Bask in the Son; feel the warmth of His love flood your heart.

I am writing the Amplified Bible's version of Deuteronomy 6:4-7. Read it carefully; then begin to apply it "first" in your own heart and mind.

JOURNAL

_____

_____

_____

_____

"But as for you, continue to hold to the things you have learned and of which you are convinced, knowing from whom you have learned them, and how from your childhood you have had a knowledge of and been acquainted with the sacred writings, which are able to instruct you and give you the understanding for salvation which comes through faith in Christ Jesus [that is, through the leaning of the entire human personality on God in Christ Jesus in absolute trust and confidence in His power, wisdom, and goodness]."

—2 Timothy 3:14,15

READING 43

Have you ever stopped to think about all the things you have learned? Having gone to a public school, I learned I was the offspring of an ape, that sex before marriage was good as long as I didn't get pregnant or give birth, and that 2+2=4. Of all the information I learned, I am convinced of only one thing—2+2=4!

Now I am the teacher, and our children have been taught many things. They too are convinced that 2+2 is still 4, that God created the heavens and the earth, that marriage is God's idea and sex begins after marriage, and that babies are the blessings of that union. They are convinced that Jesus is the only begotten Son of God, was born of a virgin, was crucified for our sins, rose from the dead and is seated at the right hand of God, interceding for them.

Has home schooling made the difference? Yes! I am convinced that it has. Because we are home schooling, our children are acquainted with the sacred writings; they understand salvation, and they know from whom they have learned these things. We have a special bond between us that exists only between parents and children, and home schooling has only strengthened that bond. As they mature and grow into godly teens, they will draw from the teachings they have grown up with. Choosing lifelong mates will be easier for them because of the standards God has laid down for them.

Home schooling is an awesome responsibility, but so is parenting. I am convinced that both are God's idea, and He blesses those that follow Him. Home schooling our children has been, and is, such a blessing.

JOURNAL

_____

_____

_____

_____

_____

_____

_____

_____

_____

"And he shall be like a tree firmly planted [and tended] by the streams of water, ready to bring forth his fruit in its season; his leaf also shall not fade or wither, and everything he does shall prosper [and come to maturity]."

—*Psalms 1:3*

READING 44

Our avocado tree is about 14 inches high. One of the first things we did, upon arriving in Florida, was to get an avocado seed to plant. It was given to us by the director of the Fruit and Spice Park, a national park filled with tropical trees.

We watched with great excitement as the roots began to seek out the water they needed to cause the tree to grow. We were awed by the speed in which the tree sprang from its seed. Before we knew it, our water-drinking tree had other needs, so we planted it in a coffee can. A new season of growth began. It still needed the water, but it needed the nutrients from the soil and the sunshine.

It is a very healthy tree and it has an abundance of foliage; however, it doesn't have any avocados yet. It would be foolish for us to expect a 14-inch avocado tree to bear mature avocados. If our little tree tried to support the weight of a single avocado, it would break.

Likewise, we must remember that the season for our children to bear fruit has not arrived yet. It will. You can be sure of it, and I believe a hundred-fold response is highly probable. After all, home schooling has provided them with the best nutrients, plenty of water, the right amount of exposure to the elements to strengthen them but not harm them, and someone to tend them with great measures of love.

As we feed them the nutrients they need for growing, remember not to demand a harvest the moment you plant the seed. Expect the harvest; it will come in due season, as long as we give them the right measure of ingredients at the proper time. Tend them with care and watch them blossom in the love of your home school.

JOURNAL

_____

_____

_____

_____

_____

_____

_____

_____

_____

"Who shall ever separate us from Christ's love? Shall suffering and affliction and tribulation? Or calamity and distress? Or persecution or hunger or destruction or peril or sword?"

—Romans 8:35

READING 45 Our children have many questions, and we don't always have the answers. Whether war occurs in the Middle East such as Desert Storm, in Europe like the conflict in Bosnia, or in the inner cities of our nation as gangs confront other gangs, war is deadly, the cost is great and the outcome is in the hands of the Almighty. As Desert Storm reared its monstrous head, I am glad that their questions came to their father and not to a teacher with conflicting thoughts. After all, their dad knew the real cost of this war and the real reasons, better than most.

As they ask him, "Do you have to go?" I hold my breath, while Christ holds our hearts. He answers, "I don't know. But I have to be ready." He is packing his bag. It will remain in our closet until it is needed. We wait on the Lord. We talk about the possibilities. Our hearts are torn between wanting our "principal" to stay here and wondering if there are enough Christians over there to minister to the fears in the foxhole. Only the Lord knows where he is most needed and most effective.

For years we have prepared ourselves for this possibility; for years we have known this is Daddy's job. For years we have prayed for the Return of the Lord. We have always known the cost of both of these events. Yet there is a peace in our home, a gentle spirit, a deep love, because we know that Chapter 8 of Romans doesn't leave us with questions. It ends with answers.

Our response should always be on our knees in prayer. Pray for those in authority over us. Pray for foreign powers and governments. Pray for our children. Pray. The prayers of the righteous avail much.

JOURNAL

"*For which of you, wishing to build a farm building, does not first sit down and calculate the cost, whether he has sufficient means to finish it? Otherwise when he has laid the foundation and is unable to complete [the building], all who see it began to mock and jeer at him, saying, this man began to build, and was not able [worth enough] to finish.*"

—*Luke 14:28-30*

READING 46 Upon hearing the news that we were expecting our first child, how many of us sat down and calculated the cost: staying home to rear our child, quitting our jobs, figuring out how old we would be when that child leaves the nest, calculating our own abilities to rear that child? If we are not careful, fear can set in and spoil the joy of the gift we have received from God.

When our children began public school, I didn't know there were costs to count. They were five years old, and that meant that they went to school. The cost was dear, too dear to continue paying, for such shoddy workmanship. Praise the Lord, He does replace what the locusts have eaten.

Counting the cost of teaching our children at home began with another list of "give-ups." I gave up morning coffee at my neighbor's, the women's Bible study I taught, and various other social activities, including lengthy telephone calls. Yet the cost was not as dear as losing our children to foreign gods.

Now as we begin another year of home schooling, as I become a junior and senior high school teacher, I scope out "this building." The foundation is so well laid, with Jesus as its cornerstone, and the pillars are strong. I can build on and on.

We have calculated the costs, have encountered jeers along the way, such as Noah must have endured while building the Ark. We have a great joy in seeing this work to completion. I encourage you to enjoy the building process. Once the foundation of elementary education is laid, the building is erected with such speed that you will be amazed at the young adult that sits across the table from you. Carry on!

JOURNAL

"Even a child is known by his acts, whether or not what he does is pure and right."

—*Proverbs 20:11*

READING 47

Today I was watching our son as he played with the neighborhood children. As I watched, I began to wonder what the other neighborhood parents thought of my child. What were his actions saying about him? Did he give them an opportunity to see his heart today? Did I take time out of my day to see his heart? The actions of my son open doors to his character. Each door that opens gives everyone a glimpse of the man he is becoming.

He made sure that the little three-year-old next door had an opportunity to hit the baseball, even though he had to pitch the ball ten times before he hit it. Did anyone else see the man inside him that will deal fairly with others? He also broke up a fight between a couple of five-year-olds: "blessed are the peace-makers." I also wonder if the others saw how he was sharing his most prized possession with the other children; he has such a giving nature. Did they also see him stomp his feet when I called him to come inside? When I don't get my own way, do I stomp my feet also? Perhaps he has watched me stomp my feet a time or two. The Proverbs say even a child is known by his actions. Does this apply to the parents of the child as well? Perfection is a long way off, but as I look at my children at play, I see the beginning of a great man and woman of God and a few areas that need to be pruned in all of us.

Open our eyes, Lord, to see the work you are doing in our hearts. Open our hands as we reach out to help others along Your path, and fill our mouths with praise.

God isn't finished with us yet, but isn't it grand to see the work of His hand in the lives of our children?

JOURNAL

_____

_____

_____

_____

_____

_____

_____

_____

_____

_____

"I have no greater joy than this, to hear that my [spiritual] children are living their lives in the Truth."

—3 John 4

READING 48 Tears flowed softly, quietly down her cheeks. Words came slowly and painfully as she tried to explain her present emotions.

"I have been so selfish, so disobedient. Nothing seems right. I love Jesus so much, but I have been so distant from Him. Mom, it hurts so much. Please, will you pray with me?"

What an honor! How grateful I am to know that she comes to me with her deepest pains, her greatest joys. Today I have the privilege of knowing both extremes, the pain of sin and the joy of restoration.

"My life just hasn't been honoring to Jesus! But I want to be a blessing to Him. I want to show everyone that Jesus is the light and love of my life. I don't want to put my light under a basket when the neighborhood kids are around. I want to begin again."

Together we pray, cry, and watch the miracle that takes place as the blood of Jesus washes a tender, hurting heart. Healing comes. How gracious our Lord is; how free she feels. Laughing, skipping like a new lamb in the spring, she leaves her prayer closet, restored. She once again is our "Joyful Spirit," which is what "Heather" means. Her first action to follow this miracle is to call the Christian radio station during "Youth Check-In." She tells everyone that she has rededicated her life to Christ.

Home schooling has its privileges and every once in awhile its blessings. What a joy it is to be home and available.

JOURNAL

_____

_____

_____

_____

_____

_____

_____

_____

_____

_____

_____

_____

_____

"But we [ourselves] cannot help telling what we have seen and heard."

—Acts 4:20

READING 49

"Your children go to school, where? At home? Would you tell me about it some-time? That is really amazing!"

Just like a baby Christian, we expound on the joys of home schooling. The baby Christian says, "See what the Lord has done for me! He has turned my life around. He can do the same for you. Let me tell you all about it!"

The home schooling parent says, "You wouldn't believe the difference it has made in our home. The children have really turned around. For the first time, I really understand what the Lord had in mind for the family. Let me tell you all about it! It will make a difference in your home, too."

Somehow we just can't help ourselves. When we have discovered something as incredible as home schooling, something that feels so natural and brings about such imme-diate results, how can we keep it to ourselves? We are just so overjoyed that we have to shout it to the world!

"Jesus is blessing our family. Quick! Come and see! Our children are laughing, skipping, reading, learning, and prais-ing the Lord. God has blessed us exceedingly."

JOURNAL

"When Jesus raised up He said to her, 'Woman, where are your accusers? Has no man condemned you?' She answered, 'No one, Lord!' And Jesus said, 'I do not condemn you either. Go on your way, and from now on sin no more.'"

–John 8:10-11

READING 50 Home schooling has benefits you cannot find in a textbook. For years now, having our children home has continually bared their hearts, and ours, too. However, there was one secret I had not been able to bring into the light. Fear of rejection is a formidable enemy, and I wasn't sure I wanted to meet him.

I have written editorials for our local newspapers, full of statistics and facts, trying to sway the hearts of the people. After years of writing in such an antiseptic manner, the Lord asked me to expose the truth by opening up my life. My arguments were fine ones: "My children don't know; if I had told them as babies, it would be different, but how can I tell them now? I'm sure it won't make any difference to the readers, Lord — they don't know me. Why now?"

So I sat down with my husband, and we talked about my life. We had always decided that when the time came, he would talk to the children. Initial reactions can be so painful. After I told him what I believed I had to do, he agreed. He would sit them down after church and talk to them. I wrote them a letter, and he would read it to them. It would be okay. He is so wonderful.

As they assembled in the living room, I washed the dishes from lunch. Tears flowed freely into the dishwater;

my hands, my whole body, were shaking. "Oh Lord, I can't lose them, too. Please help them understand!"

An hour later, our children came into the kitchen, threw their arms around me, and we cried. They were not angry. They didn't hate me. Matthew said, "I love you, Mom. I'm sorry you had to go through that." Heather said, "Mommy, why didn't you tell us sooner? We could have been praying for you. We love you so much!" Jesus said, "Trust me, I know their hearts better than you." I don't know how long they held me in their arms; I only know there is no fear in love.

All the years of training them to have compassion on sinners, teaching them to pray for strangers, and reaching out to the lost, have really paid off. They reached out to me. Later, Heather said to me these words: "Every Wednesday when we prayed for the women that had abortions, that must have been hard for you. We would have prayed for you, too. But, Mom, I have always known, because sometimes I dream about my big sister. Now I understand! I can hardly wait to meet her. I really do love you, Mom."

The Lord was right, and so was the timing. I wrote the articles. The response was incredible. A week later I was asked to speak to the Junior/Senior Class at our local high school. My children told me to accept the invitation, even though some of my daughter's friends would be attending.

They said that these students needed to hear the truth about abortion. So I went. The truth has set me free, and there really is no condemnation for those who are in Christ Jesus.

JOURNAL

_____

_____

_____

_____

_____

_____

_____

_____

_____

_____

_____

_____

_____

_____

_____

_____

"Her children rise up and call her blessed [happy, fortunate, and to be envied]; and her husband boasts of and praises her, saying, 'Many daughters have done virtuously, nobly, and well [with strength of character that is steadfast in goodness] but you excel them all.'"

—*Proverbs 31:28-29*

READING **51** The Proverbs 31 woman is my idol. This woman is my vision, my goal, as she is for most Christian women. Many studies on this mother have been written and taught. My Bible says, "With God all things are possible." So I have come to the conclusion that being a Proverbs 31 woman is possible with Christ.

When my husband suggested that I teach our children at home, he was saying, "I trust you, and I am confident in your abilities." He knew it would mean making sacrifices, cutting costs in a number of ways. He was sure I would manage, and we are.

Until I began teaching our children at home, they really were not aware of all the responsibilities of a homemaker. They were being given the modern mindset that says a woman must work outside the home in order to have value. They no longer believe this. They see all that I do to make our house a home.

The other day our daughter said that she would rather have school at home with her mother than go to school anywhere else. In her very special way, she was calling me blessed. Proverbs 31 is possible, and home schooling is helping to make it a reality in my life.

JOURNAL

_____

_____

_____

_____

_____

_____

_____

_____

_____

_____

_____

_____

_____

_____

_____

_____

_____

_____

_____

_____

_____

_____

"But Mary was keeping within herself all these things [sayings], weighing and pondering them in her heart."

—Luke 2:19

READING 52

I came across a pair of booties, small and white. The ribbons were unraveling, and the colors in the stitching were no longer vibrant. I remember the day that we saw the little moccasin kit in the leather-goods store. Mike could hardly wait to begin molding these tiny soft booties for our first-born. I still see the glistening moist green eyes that told me he had seen our precious child when she was born. It took awhile for her to grow into the gift her daddy had made for her.

This small discovery brings on a rush of memories, some treasured, some not very pleasant. Like Mary, I have much to ponder in my heart. I realize that this may seem a strange topic when discussing home education, but it really is a subject to consider.

I have much to ponder in my heart. Unlike the mothers that work outside the home, I saw my baby's first smile, first tooth, and first fever. I felt the unnatural pull of the school bus as it snatched our children away. And I remember our first day of home school. Since that time, many memories have planted themselves in my heart. Many of these times would not have occurred, had our children been walled up in a classroom for six or more hours a day. Our deep thought-provoking conversations would have been handled in a classroom by someone not familiar with my daughter's tenderness of heart. Instead, I was the first person she told when she discovered how cute the boy was who used to call her "chicken little."

This is the blessing of home schooling. Home schooling is life while it's happening and precious memories when the children are grown. How fast they grow! Thank you Lord. Your plan really is rewarding!

JOURNAL

_____

_____

_____

_____

_____

_____

_____

_____

JOURNAL